BIG ENGLISH

2ND EDITION

STUDENT'S BOOK

with online resources

2

Pearson Education Limited
KAO Two
KAO Park
Harlow
Essex CM17 9NA
England
and Associated Companies throughout the world.

www.English.com/BigEnglish2

© Pearson Education Limited 2017

First published 2017

ISBN: 978-1-292-20359-1

Set in Heinemann Roman

Printed in Italy by L.E.G.O. S.p.A.

Acknowledgements

The publisher would like to thank the following for their kind permission to reproduce their photographs:
(Key: b-bottom; c-centre; l-left; r-right; t-top)

123RF.com: 1enchik 36b/c, 4c/7, 4cl/5, 7tr, 13tc, 13tr, 17tl, 20bl, 24t, 27c, 28tr/4, 28cr/7, 32b, 33tc, 35, 35l, 35cl, 36tl/1, 36tr/4, Alexander Pokusay 11cr, andreadonetti 8tr/4, Andrey Makurin 32l, ANDRII GLUSHCHENKO 35tr, Anna Kondrateva 36b/a, Arak Rattanawijittakorn 35c, ayelet keshet 23tr/5, bbtreesubmission 11tr/5, 11c, belchonock 8tl/1, bloodua 9b, blueringmedia 7, 7t, 7tl, 7tc, 19cl/2, 20bc, 21b, 32r, 35 (Camel), 35tl (Raccoon), Cathy Yeulet 10b, Charlie Milsom 36t/3, dedmazay 19t, Dian Permana 23tl/1, Dmitrii Bachtub 16tr/4, dolgachov 7bl, 15cl, 15cr, 23bl, 23br, 39cl, 39cr, dykyostudio 16cl/5, Fernando Gregory Milan 20cr/8, fotointeractiva 37t, Gary Nicolson 36b/d, gelia 22b, gelpi 11br, 19bl, 27br, 35r, IIdar Galeev 29b, iimages 23cl/3, 23cr/6, 27t (Xena), 27tl (Jake), 27tc (Jill), Ijupco 20cl/6, indomercy 23c/8, 32br, inhabitant 16tl/1, Iryna Novytsky 37b, Ivan Mateev 30bl, Jakkarin Rongkankeaw 19c, Janaka Dharmasena 24tl/1, jovannig 26b, Jozsef Szasz-Fabian 24tl/2, Kjersti Jorgensen 34b, kopitinphoto 25tr, Kseniya Hunina 33b, lehui 37tr, Leung Cho Pan 38b, macrovector 12b, mandy godbehear 9tl, Mark Brazier 8tc/3, Mauro Rodriques 18br, monticello 24tc/3, Muhammad Destra Laksana 27tr (Luis), myibean 9tc, Oksana Duboshina 35b, Oleh Tokarev 19cl/1, Olga Traskevych 16t/2, petovarga 19cr, Prometeus 7cl, radub85 39t, ramcreative 36b/b, rawpixel 37c, rvvlada 12bl, Scott Griessel 20tr/4, serezniy 28cr/8,, sergein 31cl, silantiy 17b, Solarus 35cr, subbotina 20cl/5, Sujono sujono 23tr/4, Teguh Mujiono 9br, 11t, 23l/2, 27tr (Bart), tomaccojc 11tl, tomophotography 37tl, Vaclav Volrab 35br, vilainecrevette 21t, Woojin Kim 26cr, xalanx 20tr/3, Your Rozhkov 16b, Yulia Glam 11cl; **Pearson Education Ltd:** 20b, 23c/7, Amit John 13b, Gareth Boden 29tl, Trevor Clifford 25b, 28tr/3, Coleman Yuen. Pearson Education Asia Ltd 4t/2, Arvind Singh Negi / Red Reef Design Studio. Pearson India Education Services Pvt. Ltd 20br, Sanjay Charadva. Pearson India Education Services Pvt. Ltd 25bl, Rafal Trubisz. Pearson Central Europe SP. Z.O.O. 8cl/5; **Shutterstock.com:** 2117717 16t/3, 245188 33tl, 70sphotography 36cl/5, Alan49 36t/2, Alex Staroseltsev 13t, Alina Ku-Ku 24cr/8, Atiketta Sangasaeng 12tl/1, benchart 12br, bigacis 28tl/2, BKingFoto 29tr, bluehand 12tc/3, Brian A Jackson 24tr/4, Christophe Testi 4tl/1, David Ashley 21tr, David Steele 32tl/1, Dean Fikar 32cl/6, DenisNata 17bl, Dima Moroz 12cr/7, docstockmedia 24cl/5, doodko 20t/2, Elnur 5tr, 36cl/6, EpicStockMedia 32cl/5, Eugene Shapovalov 4tc/3, Eva Vargyasi 28tl/1, EW CHEE GUAN 29bl, Fatih Kocyildir 4cr/8, FoxPictures 16c/6, Gary Paul Lewis 8cr/8, GermÃin Ariel Berra 24br/7, GVictoria 11bl, 19br, 27bl, 35bl, homydesign 16cr/7, Iakov Filimonov 14br, ian woolcock 32cr/8, irin-k 33tr, JonMilnes 21tl, Julia Ivantsove 8c/7, Julia Kuznetsova 13bl, Julian Rovagnati 5b, 8t/2, Kathy Burns-Millyard 4tr/4, Kletr 29tc, Krylov V. 26cl, Lemberg Vector studio 12bc, leoks 6b, Luis Louro 20tl/1, magicinfoto 36c/7, Margo Harrison 4cl/6, Milan Ilic 5tc, Milena Moiola 5br, Monika Wisniewska 20cr/7, Oleg Krugliak 25t, originalpunkt 36cr/8, Pavel L Photo and Video 12t/2, PRILL 33t, Quick Shot 32tc/3, Rafa Irusta 5tl, Rikard Stadler 25c, Rob Marmion 9tr, robuart 35tl, RonTech3000 12tr/4, Room27 12cl/5, Sergiy Bykhunenko 33, 37bl, Serhiy Shullye 28cl/5, SpeedKingz 17tr, Stephen Coburn 17tc, Steve Heap 32tr/4, Tatiana Popova 8cl/6, TijanaM 31cr, Tom Grundy 32cr/7, Tungphoto 12c/6, Valentyn Volkov 28c/6, VisionDive 21tc, vovan 24cl/6, Willyam Bradberry 32tl/2, Yaping 13tl

Stickers

123RF.com: 1enchik, Fernando Gregory Milan, fotointeractiva, lehui, rawpixel, Scott Griessel, serezniy, subbotina, tomophotography; Pearson Education Ltd; Shutterstock.com: Atiketta Sangasaeng, bluehand, Eugene Shapovalov, Eva Vargyasi, EW CHEE GUAN, Burns-Millyard, Margo Harrison, Milan Ilic, Monika Wisniewska, RonTech3000, Serhiy Shullye

All other images © Pearson Education

Illustrated by Sally Whines

Every effort has been made to trace the copyright holders and we apologise in advance for any unintentional omissions. We would be pleased to insert the appropriate acknowledgement in any subsequent edition of this publication.

Contents

1 Schools On The Move

Before You Watch

I will learn about classroom objects, activities and different schools.

1 Listen, look, and say.

 1 pencil

 2 textbook

 3 internet

 4 computer

 5 board

 6 desk

 7 pen

 8 notebook

2 Complete with the words from 1.

3 Listen, look, and say.

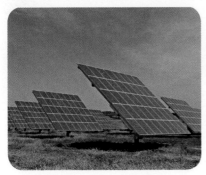

solar panels

architect

plastic bottles

4 Imagine your dream school. Where is it? How do you travel to it? What does it have? Say with a partner. Draw.

5 **Watch and stick in order. Then say.**

1	2	3	4

6 **Watch again. Match.**

a a floating classroom   United Kingdom

b a cart   Kenya

c a boat   India

d a bus   the Netherlands

7 **Read and circle. Then listen and check.**

Koen Olthuis is an **architect / engineer** from the Netherlands.
He is the designer of a classroom which floats on **fifteen /
five** thousand plastic **pencils / bottles**. The classroom teaches
children about computers.

Using plastic bottles is a fantastic way to **draw / recycle** plastic.

8 **Look at the pictures and names. Ask and answer with a partner. Use the words to help you.**

using a computer   reading a textbook   counting
coloring a picture   writing in a notebook

Carrie   **Kim and Sam**   **Ann**   **Bobby**   **Sarah**

What's Carrie doing?

She's coloring a picture.

9 **5** **Write and match. Then listen and check.**

a | What's she doing? | — | He's writing his name.

b | What _____ they _____? | | She's writing on the board.

c | What _____ he _____? | | They're using the computer.

d | What _____ she _____? | | She's reading a textbook.

THINK BIG

What are your classmates doing? Make a list.

2 Break Time

I will learn about different playground games.

 1 Listen, look, and say.

| **1** | jump rope |

| **2** | slide |

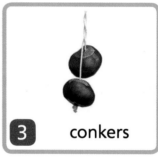

| **3** | conkers |

| **4** | Rubik's Cube |

| **5** | yo-yo |

| **6** | cards |

| **7** | swing |

| **8** | marbles |

2 Find and circle the words from **1**.

r	d	c	a	r	d	s	f	j	s
y	u	p	z	m	j	e	m	u	l
o	v	b	n	i	r	v	k	m	i
y	y	f	i	b	l	o	n	p	d
o	g	p	r	k	y	o	r	r	e
v	n	e	m	h	s	y	z	o	p
z	s	g	y	r	k	c	o	p	r
c	o	n	k	e	r	s	u	e	g
m	a	r	b	l	e	s	b	b	c
a	s	w	i	n	g	l	y	t	e

3 Listen, look, and say.

leap frog

rocking horse

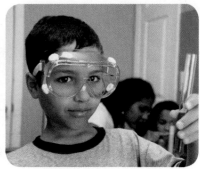

safety glasses

4 What's your favorite break time game? Ask and answer with a partner. Draw.

5 ▶ⓥ² **Watch. Check (✓) what you hear or see.**

☐ jump rope   ☐ slide   ☐ conkers
☐ Rubik's Cube   ☐ yo-yos   ☐ cards

6 ▶ⓥ² **Watch again. Match.**

a [1960s]   [cards]
b [2000]   [Rubik's Cubes]
c [1998]   [yo-yos]
d [1980]   [conkers]

7 **Read and circle. Then listen and check.**

Playground toys and **lessons / games** go in and out of fashion.
Some children still play **leapfrog / on the rocking horse** or play
on the swings.

In some schools, **conkers / slides** are back in fashion. But now,
children need to wear safety **uniforms / glasses** to play the game.

8 **Follow the maze. Ask and answer with a partner.**

Pete | Janice | Donna | Jeff | Bert

What does Pete like to do?

He likes to play on the swings.

9 **Read, listen and write. Then check.**

a Ted likes to play jump rope.

b Jane likes to _____.

c Billy and Cathy like to _____.

d George likes to _____.

THINK BIG

What do you and your classmates like to do at break time? Make a chart.

3 Sit Down!

Before You Watch

I will learn about objects to sit on.

1 Listen, look, and say.

1 chair

2 stool

3 seat

4 throne

5 couch

6 armchair

7 bed

2 Listen and number. Then write the word from 1.

3 **Listen, look, and say.**

car tire   bamboo   robot   suitcase

4 **What can you sit on at home?**
Ask and answer with a partner. Draw.

5 ▶v3 **Watch and stick in order. Then say.**

1	2	3	4

6 ▶v3 **Watch again. Match.**

a | What parks like a car? | A throne.

b | What takes eight years to make? | Bamboo.

c | What's used to make chairs in Egypt? | A tree chair.

d | What do you need if you are important? | A robot chair.

7 **Read and circle. Then listen and check.**

Making a chair is not **easy / difficult**.
A furniture shop in Egypt uses
bamboo / robots and it takes
eight weeks / one week to make a chair.
Bamboo is great for making chairs because
it's very **weak / strong**. Bamboo chairs are
very pretty.

8 **Match for you. Then ask and answer with a partner.**

Where are the stools?

They're in the kitchen!

9 **Write the words in order. Then listen and check.**

a green - in - the - kitchen - is - chair - The.
The green chair is in the kitchen.

b is - stool - The - bamboo - bathroom - in - the.

_____

c The - living - in - armchair - is - the - room.

_____

d is - bed - The - in - bedroom - the.

_____

Design a chair using only recycled materials.
Draw a picture and tell the class.

4 The Tuk-Tuk

Before You Watch

I will learn about transport and a special taxi.

15
1 Listen, look, and say.

1 wheels

2 lights

3 taxi

4 door

5 scooter

6 electric car

7 steering wheel

2 Label the picture with words from 1.

a _____

b _____

_____

c _____

d _____

3 Listen, look, and say.

driver

passenger

owner

4 What taxis do you have in your hometown? Ask and answer with a partner. Draw.

5 ▶v4 **Watch. Check (✓) what you hear or see.**

☐ taxi ☐ scooter ☐ wheel ☐ electric ☐ doors

6 ▶v4 **Watch again. Match.**

a | women-only | | India |

b | angry elephant | | Gaza |

c | shops | | Sri Lanka |

d | polo | | Pakistan |

7 **Read and circle. Then listen and check.**

There are factories that make **shop / electric** tuk-tuks. These tuk-tuks need to be **safe / fast**. Tuk-tuks have only **two / three** wheels, so they are sometimes difficult to **drive / sit**. It can be quite dangerous in the snow.

8 **Follow the maze. Ask and answer with a partner.**

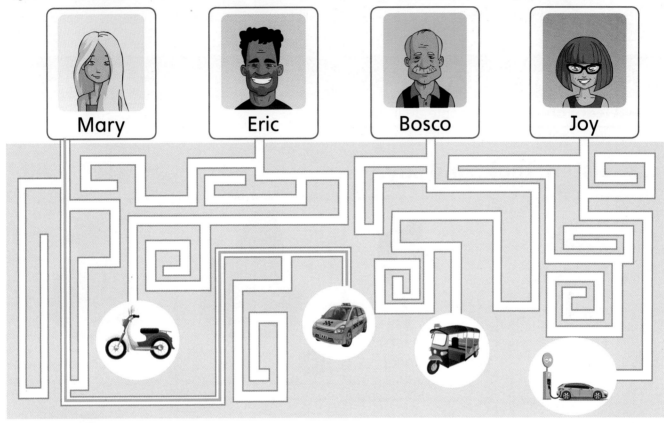

Mary   Eric   Bosco   Joy

 What does Mary want?

She wants to go by taxi.

9 **Look and match. Then listen and check.**

18

a	Is there a steering wheel?	No, there's only one door.
b	Are there lights?	Yes, there is.
c	Are there four doors?	Yes, there are.
d	Are there four wheels?	No, there are three.

 THINK BIG

Who in your class wants to be a passenger in a tuk-tuk? A driver? An owner? Make a chart.

5 Exciting Jobs

I will learn about what people do in their jobs.

1 Listen, look, and say.

1 explorer

2 dancer

3 writer

4 archaeologist

5 photographer

6 cyclist

7 vet

8 astronaut

2 **Match and write with words from 1.**

  a I want to work with animals.
  b I want to write a book.
  c I want to go to space.
  d I want to take pictures.

☐ _____   ☐ _____

☐ _____   ☐ _____

Stickers

1 **Schools On The Move** page 6

3 **Sit Down!** page 14

5 **Exciting Jobs** page 22

Stickers

7 **Food Festivals** page 30

9 **Celebrations** page 38

3 **Listen, look, and say.**

scuba diving   seabed   shark   whale

4 **Which do you think is the most exciting job? Ask and answer with a partner. Draw.**

5 ▶ V5 **Watch and stick in order. Then say.**

1	2	3	4

5 ▶ V5 **Watch again. Write.**

> archaeologist   photographer   vet   astronaut

a Who practices to go to space?   An _____.

b Who decorates a water tank?   A _____.

c Who finds secret cities on the seabed?   An _____.

d Who sees a whale?   A _____.

21

7 **Read and circle. Then listen and check.**

There are many secret
underwater / overwater cities in
seas and lakes around the world.
Archaeologists / Astronauts in
the Ukraine found the remains
of one **ancient / new** city. They
study the city to learn about
life in the past and they take
photographs / practice of what
they see.

8 Complete with the correct jobs. Ask and answer with a partner.

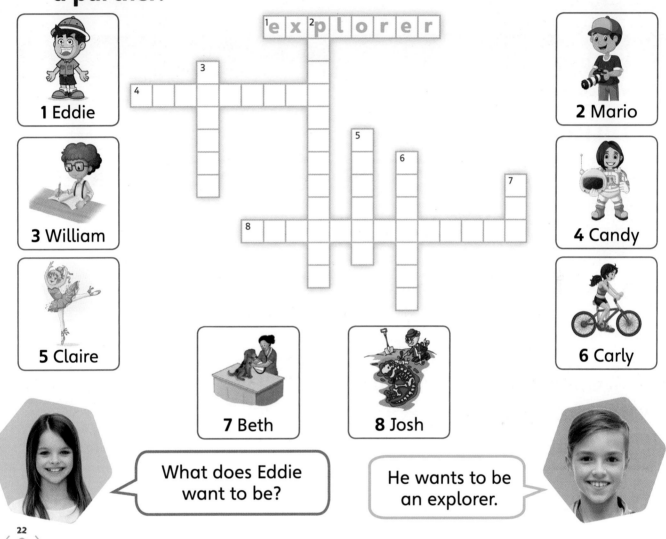

1 Eddie

2 Mario

3 William

4 Candy

5 Claire

6 Carly

7 Beth

8 Josh

What does Eddie want to be?

He wants to be an explorer.

9 Read and write. Then listen and check.

a Amy likes animals. She wants to be a vet.

b Brendon likes to ride his bike. _____

c Mark likes to take photographs. _____

d Jenna likes to read about the planets. _____

_____

THINK BIG

What do you and your classmates want to be? Make a list.

What Time Is It?

I will learn about telling the time.

 1 **Listen, look, and say.**

1 second

2 minute

3 hour

4 day

5 week

6 month

7 year

8 calendar

2 **Find and circle the words from 1.**

h	o	u	r	n	x	x	y	s	w	v	d
c	t	g	e	z	m	i	n	u	t	e	t
a	a	x	m	s	p	i	p	n	a	h	j
l	j	j	l	l	v	y	j	r	n	d	q
e	o	s	u	n	s	e	t	i	m	a	y
n	r	f	k	a	a	a	h	s	j	y	w
d	c	l	w	s	f	r	v	e	n	m	e
a	q	q	w	e	e	k	x	c	x	o	g
r	l	i	m	c	x	b	c	d	w	n	f
w	h	s	i	o	x	u	g	c	g	t	a
d	h	x	e	n	s	y	y	o	a	h	w
y	h	w	g	d	y	a	i	a	m	a	o

3 **Listen, look, and say.**

cuckoo clock   mechanical clock   digital clock   watch

4 **What do you use to tell the time?**
Ask and answer with a partner. Draw.

Watch. Check (✓) what you hear or see.

☐ hours ☐ days ☐ weeks ☐ years
☐ cuckoo clocks ☐ watches ☐ calendar ☐ digital clocks

6 ▶v6 **Watch again. Match.**

Stonehenge

Water Clock

☐ 600 years ago

☐ shortest day

☐ bells

☐ metal balls

☐ calendar

☐ stones

7 **Read and circle. Then listen, and check.**

Many people believe that Stonehenge is a solar **calendar / watch**.
This is because the way the sun shines on Stonehenge changes

through the **minute / year**.
On the shortest **hour / day**
of the year, as it rises, the
sun / moon shines through
a gap in the stones. And on
the longest day of the year,
it shines through a different
gap.

8 **Follow the lines. Say with a partner.**

Jake   Xena   Jill   Luis   Bart

What time does Jake brush his teeth?

He brushes his teeth at 6:00.

9 **Write and match. Then listen and check.**

26

a When **does** she brush her teeth?   School starts at 9:00.

b When _____ school start?   They eat dinner at 7:00.

c When _____ school end?   School ends at 4:00.

d When _____ they eat dinner?   She brushes her teeth at 8:00.

THINK BIG

What's your favorite time of the day? Why? Tell a partner.

7 Food Festivals

I **will learn about** food and food festivals.

27
1 Listen, look, and say.

1 pumpkins

2 Brussels sprouts

3 radishes

4 bananas

5 avocados

6 beans

7 cherries

8 strawberries

2 Complete with the words from 1.

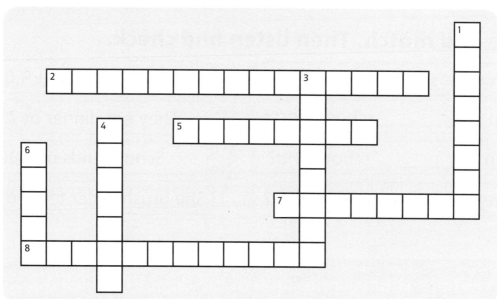

28

3 **Listen, look, and say.**

carve

harvest

ripe

4 **What are the food festivals near you?**
Ask and answer with a partner. Draw.

 Watch and stick in order. Then say.

1	2	3	4

5 ▶ **v7** **Watch again. Match.**

a | bananas | | Morocco
b | strawberries | | United Kingdom
c | Brussels sprouts | | India
d | cherries | | Ivory Coast

 Read and circle. Then listen and check.

The Night of the Radishes is an event in the city of Oaxaca in **Mexico / Morocco**. It takes place every year. Farmers carve big **radishes / pumpkins** into figures and scenes. The event is a very popular tradition. They can make anything out of a radish: a sea monster, a **farmer / cowboy**, or even a train!

8 **Follow the maze. Ask and answer with a partner.**

Does Todd like beans?

No, he doesn't. He likes avocados

9 **Read and write. Then listen and check.**

a Does she like **strawberries**? Yes, she **does**. She likes strawberries.

b Does he _____ cherries? No, he doesn't. He _____ bananas.

c _____ she like Brussels sprouts? No, she _____ like Brussels sprouts. She likes beans and radishes.

d Do they _____ pumpkin? Yes, they _____ They like avocados, too.

What do you like? What do your classmates like? Make a chart.

8 Where Animals Live

Before You Watch

I will learn about animals and their habitats.

 1 Listen, look, and say.

1 desert

2 ocean

3 jungle

4 city

5 forest

6 farm

7 river

8 lake

2 Write with words from 1.

a Sharks live in the _____.

b Camels live in the _____.

c Cows live on a _____.

d Tigers live in the _____.

32

3 **Listen, look, and say.**

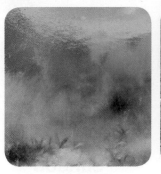   

| algae | raccoon | lizard | bugs |

4 **What animals can you find where you live?**
Ask and answer with a partner. Draw.

5 ▶ v8 **Watch. Check (✓) what you hear or see.**

☐ desert ☐ lizard ☐ ocean ☐ algae
☐ raccoons ☐ cities ☐ iguana ☐ bugs

5 ▶ v8 **Watch again. Match.**

a | marine iguana | | Canada |

b | shovel snouted lizard | | Galapagos |

c | raccoon | | Namibia |

7 33 **Read and circle. Then listen and check.**

The Namibian Desert is a **cold / hot** place to live. The shovel snouted lizard stands on **two / one** legs because it's too hot. It dives **on / under** the sand to find bugs to eat.

In the Galapagos, some lizards go to the **ocean / forest** to find food. They eat **algae / fish** on the rocks.

8 **Follow the lines. Ask and answer with a partner.**

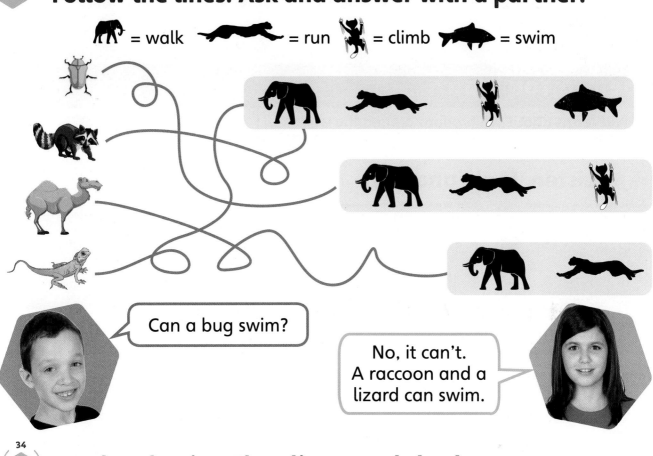

= walk   = run   = climb   = swim

Can a bug swim?

No, it can't.
A raccoon and a
lizard can swim.

34

9 **Read and write. Then listen and check.**

climb   live   swim   like   ~~run~~

What do you know about tigers?

Tigers can **run** very fast and they can _____
trees. They can _____, too! In fact, tigers are
good swimmers and they _____ to swim in
rivers and lakes! Tigers don't live in the ocean.
They _____ in forests and jungles.

THINK BIG   What other animals can walk, run, climb, and swim?
Can any animals talk? Check the internet.

Celebrations

I will learn about celebrations around the world.

35

 1 **Listen, look, and say.**

1 costumes	**2** lanterns

3 parade

4 fireworks

5 festival

6 masks

7 balloons

8 confetti

2 **Write with words from 1.**

a We bring _____.

b The _____ are very loud.

c We put on _____ to cover our faces.

d We watch the _____.

3 Listen, look, and say.

| Mid-Autumn Festival | Day of the Dead | Independence Day | Chinese New Year |

4 What do people do at New Year in your country? Ask and answer with a partner. Draw.

5 ▶ⁿ **Watch and stick in order. Then say.**

| 1 | 2 | 3 | 4 |

6 ▶ⁿ **Watch again. Answer Yes or No.**

a Is the Day of the Dead festival in the USA? _____

b Are there parades on Independence Day? _____

c Is Chinese New Year sometimes in January? _____

d Is Chinese New Year only celebrated in China? _____

7 🎧37 **Read and circle. Then listen and check.**

All around the world, people have special **months / days** for celebration. They take place throughout the year. May Day is celebrated in many countries in Europe and North **America / Asia**. In Eastern Asia the Mid-Autumn **Festival / Day** is a popular **celebration / year**.

8 **Follow the maze. Ask and answer with a partner. Use always.**

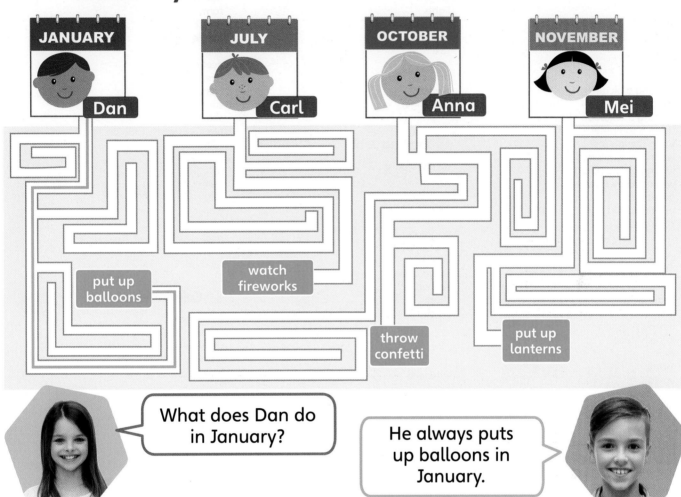

JANUARY — Dan

JULY — Carl

OCTOBER — Anna

NOVEMBER — Mei

put up balloons

watch fireworks

throw confetti

put up lanterns

What does Dan do in January?

He always puts up balloons in January.

9 **Match and write always or never. Then listen and check.**

38

a | What does she do in January?

b | Does he have a Chinese New Year's party in June?

c | Do people wear masks on Independence Day?

d | Do they wear costumes and masks in October?

No, they _____ wear masks on Independence Day.

She **always** has a New Year's party in January.

Yes, they _____ wear costumes and masks in October.

No, he _____ has a Chinese New Year's party in June.

THINK BIG

What's your favorite holiday? What do you do? Make a list and tell your classmates.

Word List

1 Schools on the Move

board
computer
desk
internet
notebook
pen
pencil
textbook
coloring a picture
counting
reading a textbook
using a computer
using the internet
writing in a notebook
writing on the board
writing his/her name
architect
plastic bottles
solar panels

2 Break Time

cards
conkers
jump rope
marbles
Rubik's Cube
slide
swing
yo-yo
play cards
play conkers
play jump rope
play marbles
play on the slide
play on the swings
play with a Rubik's Cube
play with a yo-yo
leapfrog
rocking horse
safety glasses

3 Sit Down!

armchair
bed
chair
couch
seat
stool
throne
bathroom
bedroom
kitchen
living room
leapfrog
rocking horse
safety glasses
bamboo
car tire
robot
suitcase

4 The Tuk-Tuk

door
electric car
lights
scooter
steering wheel
taxi
wheels
driver
owner
passenger

5 Exciting Jobs

archaeologist
astronaut
cyclist
dancer
explorer
photographer
vet
writer
scuba diving
seabed
shark
whale

6 What Time Is It?

calendar
day
hour
minute
month
second
week
year
brush his/her teeth
eat breakfast
eat dinner
get up
go to bed
go to school
cuckoo clock
digital clock
mechanical clock
watch

7 Food Festivals

avocados
bananas
beans
Brussels sprouts
cherries
pumpkins
radishes
strawberries
carve
harvest
ripe

8 Where Animals Live

city
desert
farm
forest
jungle
lake
ocean
river
camel
cow
shark
tiger
climb
find food
run
swim
talk
walk
algae
bugs
lizard
raccoon

9 Celebrations

balloons
confetti
costumes
festival
fireworks
lanterns
masks
parade
always
never
sometimes
Chinese New Year
Day of the Dead
Independence Day
Mid-Autumn Festival